CATH
T

A Way In

by

Stratford Caldecott

Plater College, Oxford

All booklets are published thanks to the generous support of the members of the Catholic Truth Society

CATHOLIC TRUTH SOCIETY
PUBLISHERS TO THE HOLY SEE

CONTENTS

What is Catholic Social Teaching? 5

Right and Wrong 11

Person and Society 17

The Political Order 26

Civil Society 34

Family 38

Ecology 43

Justice 48

Freedom 53

Work 56

The Commandments 61

Conclusion: Living in Christ 70

Summary of Teaching Documents 74

Bibliography 93

About This Book

There are by now many good introductions to Catholic
Social Teaching. Some of these will be found listed in the
Bibliography. Plater College in Oxford, which was founded
in 1921 by the Catholic Social Guild, has been teaching the
subject for eighty years, and during that time has tried many
different approaches. Obviously there is no single "right"
way that suits everyone. Some people prefer an historical
approach, some a doctrinal one based on the social encyclicals. Some prefer to begin with the findings of the social
sciences, others from what Scripture says, others again from
reflecting upon their own experiences of social injustice.

For that very reason, there is room for another introduction to the subject. This one also will not suit every poten-
tial reader, but it may be helpful to some. I have called it "A
Way In" because it is based on an attempt to get beyond the
technical vocabulary in which the teaching is often present-
ed. It does not seek to be exhaustive, but, by sketching the
outlines of what is known as the 'Social Gospel', it seeks to
show how this great teaching is rooted both in God's
covenant with the human race, and in plain common sense.

Stratford Caldecott
1 May 2001, St Joseph the Worker

Acknowledgements

The author would like to thank his wife and children for their patience
and support; Michael Blades, the Principal of Plater College, for his
encouragement; Andrew Abela for helpful comments on the final draft;
and Rodger Charles SJ for substantial help with last-minute revisions.

CATHOLIC SOCIAL TEACHING: AN OUTLINE

"Love the Lord with all your strength, and your neighbour as yourself" (Matt. 22:37-9)

Some Sources of Catholic Social Teaching

Natural Law
Revelation
Tradition
+ Insights from other traditions

Some Principles of Catholic Social Teaching

Person (*'personalism' vs 'Individualism'*)
    Relation to God
    Relation to neighbour
Human Society
    Society with God
    Society with neighbour
The Common Good
    Solidarity (*'social charity', 'active compassion'*)
    Subsidiarity (*empowerment, devolution, etc.*)
    Stewardship (*of natural resources*)
    Universal destination of goods (*social 'mortgage'*)
Justice (*the ordering of relationships in society*)

Some Practical Implications of Catholic Social Teaching

Priority of the Family	Equality of Women, races
Protection for Unborn and Aged	Dignity of Work
Option for the Poor	Hospitality
Limits of the Market	Forgiveness of Debt

WHAT IS CATHOLIC SOCIAL TEACHING?

In recent years, particularly during the pontificate of Pope John Paul II, which began in 1978, Catholic Social Teaching has won wide acclaim and serious attention among other Christians, among followers of other religions, and even among those who do not believe in God. This may have begun with the fall of Communism in Europe in the 1980s, and the key role played by the Pope from Poland in that great historical drama; but whatever the reasons, these teachings have come to be recognized by many as more sensible and more balanced, more nuanced and more sophisticated, than the political ideologies associated with both Communism and Capitalism. At a time when politics often seems to be less about 'big ideas' than about getting elected, Catholic Social Teaching seems to offer hope that realism and idealism may not be incompatible after all.

What it is Not

The social teaching of the Church is that part of her moral theology which is concerned with social, political and economic charity and justice. It does not, however, constitute a programme in any of these areas. Practical programmes and policies are the responsibility of statesmen and politicians to develop. These must conform to the moral law, it being the Church's role to set out what that law demands through her social teaching. John Paul II writes:

"The Church has no models to present; models that are real and effective can only arise within the framework of different historical situations, through the efforts of all those who responsibly confront concrete problems in all their social, political and cultural aspects, as these interact with each other. For such a task the Church offers her social teaching as an *indispensable and ideal orientation...* towards the common good" *(CA, 43)*. [For abbreviations, please see bibliography.] "Since it is not an ideology, the Christian faith does not presume to imprison changing socio-political realities in a rigid schema, and it recognizes that human life is realized in history in conditions that are diverse and imperfect" *(CA, 46)*. "This teaching is seen in the efforts of individuals, families, people involved in cultural and social life, as well as politicians and statesmen to give it a concrete form and application in history" *(CA, 59)*.

"The Church's social doctrine *is not* a 'third way' between *liberal capitalism* and *Marxist collectivism*, nor even a possible alternative to other solutions less radicaly opposed to one another: rather, it constitutes a *category of its own*. Nor is it an *ideology*, but rather the *accurate formulation* of the results of a careful reflection on the complex realities of human existence, in society and in the international order, in the light of faith and of the Church's tradition. Its main aim is to *interpret* these realities, determining their conformity with or divergence

from the lines of the Gospel teaching on man and his vocation, a vocation which is at once earthly and transcendent; its
aim is thus *to guide* Christian behaviour. It therefore belongs
to the field, not of *ideology*, but of *theology* and particularly
of moral theology" *(SRS, 41, see also CA, 56)*.

Strictly speaking, therefore, Catholic Social Teaching
is a set of moral principles or guidelines for action, which
have been elaborated and refined through the Church's
long dialogue with man and the problems of human society. She does not teach these principles as if from above
or outside human society, but from within it - as Christ
did - sharing with her founder an absolute commitment to
the dignity of all human beings, whose troubles and tri-
umphs she has shared for two thousand years.

These principles are rooted in the Scriptures, have
been developed by the Fathers of the Church (the first
great theologians) and their successors, clarified by councils and popes and finally summed up in the modern
"social encyclicals" and other Church documents. In all
this time Catholic thinkers have been seeking ways of
charity, justice and peace amid the world's problems, in
numerous different cultures and systems. With many of
these the Church has been in conflict, although she has
also found much to admire and from which to learn. Her
social teaching is an integral part of her conception of
life. It rests on one basic principle: human beings are the
purpose and end of every social organization.

A Teaching Whose Time Has Come

Presupposed here, as in everything the Pope writes, is the vision of Catholic vocation laid out by the Second Vatican Council in the 1960s, for example in the so-called "Pastoral Constitution on the Church in the World" entitled *Gaudium et Spes* (*"Joy and Hope"*). That is the document in which the Council Fathers explored the human condition in the mid-twentieth century, the need for Christ and the light he sheds on that condition. In it they looked at the reasons for atheism, the role of the Church, the centrality of marriage, and the intimate connection between faith and culture, economic and political life. Bishop Karol Wojtyla (later to become John Paul II) was one of those Council Fathers, and the task of his pontificate has been to consolidate and interpret the great achievements of the Council.

Catholic Social Teaching in its modern form first emerged a hundred years earlier, as a considered response to the new injustices brought about by the Industrial Revolution (the widespread exploitation of a new class of industrial labourers by a relatively small class of entrepreneurs), and also to the growing threat of class warfare made worse by the developing ideology of Communism. The Church's response to all this was summed up by Pope Leo XIII's encyclical *Rerum Novarum* (*"Of New Things"*) in 1891. This great charter inspired a whole host of Catholic and Christian social movements, and was followed by other documents which developed this teaching further and responded to the changing social conditions of the twentieth century. (You will find a summary of several of the major documents at p.74-93.) Under John Paul II, and largely thanks to his initiatives, Catholic Social Teaching not only played an important role in the final collapse of Communism in Europe, but has been extended to address the "new things" of our own day, such as globalization and the environment.

Furthermore, the teaching has been broadened and deepened by close attention to the question of *culture* on the one hand, and *Christian anthropology* on the other. Pope Paul VI and John Paul II have borne witness to the emergence of what the latter has famously called a "culture of death" in western society. This is a culture associated with materialism and consumerism, the result of which is to regard everything - including human life - merely as a means to the end of maximizing pleasure. The elderly and the unborn, in particular, tend to become regarded by such a society as inconvenient and expendable. To counter this bleak vision, Catholic Social Teaching proposes a "culture of life" and a "civilization of love": not as a utopia, but as a true social and cultural reality that begins to emerge as soon as any community of people starts to take seriously the basic principles being described in this book.

The vision of the human person or "Christian anthropology" that lies behind Catholic Social Teaching is the major factor in the Church's intellectual resistance to the culture of death. The technical details of this anthropology are beyond the scope of an introductory book, but essentially it means that a new approach to ethical and social questions has become possible: an approach that can explain the link between morality and human happiness. Alongside the "doctrinal" elements of Catholic Social Teaching a whole new field of theology is opening up: *Social Theology*, which uses Christian anthropology to explore and integrate the truths revealed in Holy Scripture and the truths discovered empirically (by observation and experiment) in the social sciences.

Sometimes we think that, just because the Second Vatican Council closed more than 30 years ago, it is no longer relevant to us. But the Church thinks in centuries. Like all Church councils throughout history, Vatican II was a product of its time. Prompted by the Holy Spirit, it set the Church on a certain course. The Church did not arrive in the Promised Land after the Council, but it has been given a direction in which to travel. That journey continues, and the adventure has barely begun.

RIGHT AND WRONG

Catholic Social Teaching hinges on the nature of the human person and the nature of human society: the good of the person and the common good. But before we examine these ideas in more detail, it is important to be clear *where the teaching comes from, and what it is based upon.* After all, the Church addresses her social teaching to everyone, not just to Catholics who may be expected to accept her right to teach them. Therefore she does not appeal solely to her own authority to justify the teaching. She appeals not just to revelation, and to her own lived tradition inspired by faith, but also to human intelligence: to basic *common sense.*

Natural Law and Conscience

She appeals, first of all, to that sense of there being an objective right and wrong which is found the world over, deep in the conscience of all human beings. Of course, we may disagree amongst ourselves on whether certain particular actions are morally good or evil, but that there is a moral good and evil is something that is evident to all. All of us, even the most liberal-minded, can be pushed to the point where we admit that certain actions (torturing children, for example) are morally unacceptable.

And in fact different races and cultures do not disagree as radically as we might think, even over the details of what counts as right and wrong. In an appendix to his little book *The Abolition of Man*, C.S. Lewis once assembled a list of the common precepts and moral principles recognized by all civilizations of all times. He called these "illustrations of the *Tao*", meaning by this what philosophers have called the "Natural Law". They included such things as fairness, honesty, respect, loyalty, filial piety, magnanimity, mercy and courage.

This Law is written deep within the human heart, and is decoded - albeit not always consistently or correctly - by the faculty called conscience. Conscience, then, is one of the realities of universal human experience on which the Catholic Church bases her social teaching. Cardinal John Henry Newman emphasized our duty always to follow our conscience in his famous *Letter to the Duke of Norfolk (1876)*, citing an ancient teaching of the Church: "He who acts against his conscience loses his soul".

But Newman also emphasized that this sovereignty of conscience does not give us a license to do whatever we may happen to feel is right at any given moment. Our conscience may be in error, and if so it is a serious matter. An error is an evil, and if the error stems from not caring enough to find out what is true and good, or from habitual sin, from needless ignorance of the Gospel, or from deliberate rejection of the Church's

teaching, it is culpable. To have a conscience is to
have a duty to "inform" or educate that conscience as
best we are able: to examine the arguments, to consider the relevant authorities, to look at the circumstances and likely outcomes of our actions, and to
weigh all of these factors intelligently. We must also
pray for guidance.

If we have done our best in all these ways to decide
what is right to do, and come to a conclusion, then we can
be sure, not that it is necessarily the right thing (for we
might still be mistaken in our judgment), but that we are
right to do it. We must take responsibility for our actions
- but also we must always remain open to the possibility
of revising our judgement if new evidence or a new argument comes to light. To act otherwise would be to betray
our own selves, and thus to betray the image of God within us. God knows we will make mistakes - even, sometimes, very costly mistakes - but he wants us always to
act with integrity, and to do our best with whatever light
he gives us. *(Cf. Catechism, 1776-1802.)*

The Virtues

Our heart does not merely inform us that one action is
right or another wrong. It indicates a moral "direction" in
which to travel. The actions of a human being cannot be
isolated from each other: every one of them is *the act of a
whole person*, and it helps to determine the course that

person is travelling - or, to put it another way, the kind of person he or she is becoming.

Every culture has ideals, and it has heroes. What it calls "virtues" are the patterns of nobility and holiness that it finds exemplified in certain individuals, and which it holds up to everyone for imitation. A hero is a kind of beacon in the dark, showing what it is possible to strive to be. At some level, we each see ourselves as the protagonist in a story - the story of a life. It is important that we strive to make that protagonist a true hero. In the words of the popular song, "you have to search for the hero inside yourself". In the Christian tradition the heroes are largely the saints, who are recognized as having successfully reached the end of their journey, their personal quest. When the Church "canonizes" someone as a saint, all she is doing is stating that she believes this person to have reached heaven. In order to be so recognized, a saint must possess "heroic virtue".

The virtues are formulated in a variety of ways, but among the most important are *Justice, Prudence, Temperance and Fortitude*. These are "Cardinal Virtues". You can think of them as something like the foundations of a building, without which the moral structure of a society will eventually collapse. These four virtues are found in the Classical as well as the Christian world, because they are based not on Revelation but on reason and conscience probing the Natural Law. Of these four virtues, Justice is perhaps the most immediately relevant to Catholic Social Teaching, if only because it is the one virtue that is primarily concerned with the ordering of relationships in society (as we shall see in more detail later).

These natural sources of social and moral reflection are heightened by Revelation. God the Creator reveals something of himself, and something about the nature of truth, by entering into an ever-deeper relationship with human beings - and ultimately by becoming human. In so doing he does not only teach us about himself: he "reveals man to himself and brings to light his most high calling" *(Gaudium et Spes, 22)*. That is, he reveals us in revealing himself. He reveals - in himself - the true source and deepest pattern of the Natural Law that we find present in ourselves when we discern good and evil.

Original Sin

But why is it necessary to make that discernment at all? Why is there evil? The prevalence of evil in the world - not to mention the difficulty of distinguishing in practice between right and wrong - is a fact of universal experience. Our intuition tells us that something is wrong, that things are "not right", not the way they were supposed to be. The Christian Revelation confirms that suspicion. The story of the "apple" (the fruit of the tree of the knowledge of good and evil, *Gen 2:17*) in the Garden of Eden may sound childish to people raised on the theory of evolution, but it tells us something we desperately need to know. Human nature (represented in the story by Adam and Eve) is *out of harmony* with the divine will that created it - and consequently in conflict with itself. We have moments of peace, moments of happiness, but we are locked in a pattern of suffering. At the root of all this suffering lies the misuse of free will. All human sins form part of an archetypal, an "original" sin, just as truly as all human individuals form part of an archetypal Man and Woman who preceded us in God's plan of creation.

When God himself took on human nature, in the person of Jesus Christ, a new archetype was created. This one human individual, being at the same time divine, was capable of joining to himself the whole human race and healing the damage that has been done by Original Sin. The tension between the two archetypes, the two "attractors" of human destiny, the two patterns that have been set for us - sin and salvation, death and life - is what history is all about. We are not compelled to choose one or the other. Everything turns on what we decide to do.

PERSON AND SOCIETY

The starting point for Catholic Social Teaching is *the human person.*

"Let us make man in our image, according to our likeness" *(Genesis 1:26).* The first or archetypal human beings, according to Scripture, were made in the "image" and the "likeness" of God. Our resemblance to God therefore lies in our very being: not merely in our intelligence, or memory, or will - let alone our outward appearance! - but in the totality of what we are. Being an *image* of God, a "child" of God, each of us is loved by him. However far we stray, God wants us to return to him. In other words, each of us has a destiny in God. This is the foundation of the idea that every human being has equal dignity with every other. It does not mean that we are "equal" in every other way - if "equal" is supposed to mean "the same". As far as intelligence, talents, looks or holiness are concerned, we are clearly very different from each other. Nevertheless, God loves us all equally, whether we are rich or poor, tall or short, beautiful or ugly, clever or stupid.

To be made in the image of God is also to have *freedom.* We are given freedom for a purpose, and the purpose is so that we may be capable of love. We are spiritual beings, made in the image of God, and "God is love" *(1 John 4:8)*. Just as a tree "must" grow and a lion "must" eat, so we *must* learn to love, for it is in the image of love that we were formed and will be perfected. This corresponds to our experience, and is celebrated in all the literature of the world. Love is the meaning of life; it is the only thing that makes life meaningful. We are called to love; but love is something that can only be given freely: it can never be forced or programmed into us. (It is worth noting that freedom exists for the sake of love, not the other way around, because in the last few hundred years we have tended to make freedom into something of an absolute).

Being free we have responsibilities. We have duties, and correspondingly others have duties towards us. This is the origin of what are called "human rights". For example, we have a right to life, and a right to respect from other people. We have many rights, and each of them corresponds to a duty, like the two sides of a coin. My duty *to respect* you is the same as your right to *be respected* by me. And I respect you primarily not because you may be handsome or talented or important, but in the first place simply because you are a person. We will look more at the idea of rights later on.

Thus we see that Catholic teaching revolves around the human person, because it revolves around love. The mystery of man is a mystery of love. It is a mystery that we will never understand completely, because we are finite and this mystery conducts us in the direction of Infinity. But at least we now know what we are and what we are doing here, thanks to the Incarnation which reveals so much to those who are willing to look and see: "it is only in the mystery of the Word made flesh that the mystery of man truly becomes clear" *(Gaudium et Spes, 22)*. The language of God is the language of personhood, and in that language he expresses what we most need to know - the one thing that only he could tell us: why we were made.

"Personalism"

The doctrine and implications of Christian Personalism are summarized beautifully in sections 355 to 361 of *The Catechism of the Catholic Church*. The implications for justice in society begin to be spelled out in section 1929.

The Common Good

To be a person, to be called to love implies that we are also part of a *society*. Persons do not exist in isolation. God is love because God is a Trinity of Persons: we say that the Father loves the Son and the Son loves the Father in the unity of the Holy Spirit. God is a Lover who gives, a Beloved who receives and a Love that is both given and received.

To be a human person is similarly to be a part of a *society*, beginning with the family into which one is born.

To be made "in the image of God" is to be made for a
loving relationship with others. To love others is to serve
them, to do them good. And because of the way we are
made, to do good to others is often the best way of doing
good for ourselves. So in order to fulfil ourselves we must
cooperate and work together to create something good for
all of us, a society that we all enjoy living in, a *common
good*. This common good, which forms one of the basic
principles of Catholic Social Teaching, is sometimes
defined as "the sum total of social conditions which
enable individuals, families and organizations to achieve
their own fulfilment more fully and easily" *(see GS, 26
and 74; Catechism, 1877-1948)*.

But society has to be *organized* in some way for this
harmony to be possible. The ordering or organization of
society is either just or unjust - that is, fair or unfair.
What we call "justice" is that state of social harmony in
which the actions of each person best serve the common
good. Catholic Social Teaching is therefore largely concerned with the question of what is just and what is
unjust. There are several different types of justice,
depending on which kind of social relationship one is
considering *(Catechism, 2411)*, but all of them play an
important part in the common good, for it is in everyone's
interest for justice to be done to all. If one person is being
unfairly treated, the fulfilment of every other person is
potentially compromised.

Solidarity and Subsidiarity

There are two other principles of Catholic Social Teaching that are closely related to the concept of the common good, although the words are of much more recent coinage: *solidarity* and *subsidiarity*. The first of these means "brotherhood" or "social charity". The word "solidarity", of course, came into the Church's vocabulary when the Polish Pope was elected in 1978, for he was a strong supporter of the trades union movement *Solidarnosc* led by Lech Walesa. But the word is a good one, for it implies a kind of social unity brought about by the free will of individuals. The *solidarity* between us is the way we share our lives with one another, so that what is good for one is also good for the others. You could call it the "horizontal" principle of social life, because it defines the way we relate together among ourselves, as equals: the way we work together, help each other, form associations of common interest, and so on.

If solidarity is the horizontal, then *subsidiarity* is the "vertical" principle of social organization. Without it, the freedom that is essential to solidarity would be in danger. We might become like members of a hive or herd, dominated by the pressures of the collective, or the will of some tyrant who could control the collective. Fallen human beings have a tendency to accumulate power. But love, by contrast, is a process of setting free, of creating space for the other. This implies that all power in a

Christian community should be exercised at the lowest and most local level compatible with the common good. There has to be a contrary force against the tendency of power to accumulate. In this way everyone is given maximum scope to exercise their own free will, and so "achieve their own fulfilment" (as our definition of the common good puts it). Thus subsidiarity describes a kind of hierarchy - but it is a hierarchy which differs from the political structures of this world in that power is continually flowing not upwards to the summit but downwards towards the base. (Jesus says: "I came not to be served but to serve.")

If you were to put both subsidiarity and solidarity together - the vertical and the horizontal in one simple image - you would have the basic symbol of Christianity: a cross. Inscribe that cross inside a circle, and you have a symbolic image of the Christian world. And, of course, the theological source of both subsidiarity and solidarity, like that of the Cross, is the Trinity. The self-giving of each divine Person empowers each of the others with maximum freedom. Each Person is free; each Person uses that freedom to give freely to the other. In the world of creatures, by analogy, subsidiarity is the principle by which each human person is rendered *as free as possible* to "own" his or her own actions: in other words, to be in a position to take responsibility for what is done and not done.

It is the common good which determines the "limits" of subsidiarity, in the sense that it is for the sake of the common

good that decisions must sometimes be taken at a higher
or less local level. My community (Oxford) might decide
it is in its own interests to dam the river Isis in order to
generate extra electricity, but what will that do to communities further down the Thames? Solidarity compels us to
take account of the effects of our actions on others, and
higher authorities must exist whose job it is to coordinate
the actions of many communities in the interests of the
common good.

The Option for the Poor

Love's reversal of worldly values and hierarchies in
favour of the Other, the neighbour, the one who is on the
margin or at the bottom of the heap, must also imply that
our actions should always be directed in such a way as to
benefit the poor rather than the rich. This is the origin of
what has come to be called since the 1970s the "preferential option for the poor". It is why Pope John Paul II in
Centesimus Annus, though critical of Marxism and its
influence on some Latin American theologians, affirms
the valuable insight at the heart of the best liberation theology, and speaks of "the positive value of an authentic
theology of integral human liberation" *(CA, 26)*.

The option for the poor is the result of these two vital
principles, solidarity and subsidiarity, working together to
create a reversal of normal worldly values. We see throughout human history that, when either principle is neglected,

society tends to revert to another pattern altogether: an "option for the rich" which is in contradiction to the Gospel.

Capitalism and Communism

In economics, as in politics, the two principles of solidarity and subsidiarity are vital to keep in balance. The economic system of communism did not work, and eventually collapsed, because of a lack of subsidiarity. The communists imposed a *controlled economy*: that is, the Party bosses decided what the various industries and factories should make, what the shops should sell, what the prices should be, and so on. But those decisions were not driven by what was needed or wanted by the people, or what was actually possible given the resources available. Furthermore it eliminated all sense of personal responsibility on the part of the workers themselves. The capitalist or "free market" system generally works better because prices and production are determined much more directly by what the consumer actually wants, and is able or willing to pay. Also, it encourages creativity on the part of those who think they may be able to make a profit for themselves making something that others will want (entrepreneurship). Capitalism therefore has "subsidiarity" in abundance, because control is exercised not from the top but rather at a local level.

But capitalism, by contrast, can fail in a different way through lack of the other principle, solidarity. Too much freedom for individuals, if that freedom is not kept in check by society at large or by the State, can lead to injustice of a different sort, but every bit as bad. By this I mean the exploitation of the weak by the strong, and the division of society (at the global as well as the national level) between the very rich and the very poor. The Bishops of England and Wales tell us in their document *Life, Debt and Jubilee (1999)* that the combined wealth of the world's 225 richest people equals the annual income of the poorest 47 per cent of the world's people! A lack of solidarity can manifest itself in many other ways, too. This is why the Pope in *Centesimus Annus* makes a point of emphasizing that the "market" has limits *(section 40)*, and must be contained by a strong "juridical framework" *(section 42)*.

THE POLITICAL ORDER

All human societies develop some kind of political structure for regulating themselves and coordinating their common activities in war and peace. Catholic Social Teaching is not wedded to any one type of political order, and the Church has worked with many political orders over the centuries, including monarchies and empires, insisting in the end only on the rule of law, whereby "the law is sovereign, and not the arbitrary will of individuals" *(CA, 33)*. The rule of law can best be maintained by balancing legislative, executive and judicial powers against each other, rather than by combining them all in one person or institution. That, at least, is the Church's best judgment based on two thousand years of history.

The principles of Catholic Social Teaching already outlined have a clear application in societies which are ruled democratically - that is, by governments elected by all citizens through a secret ballot, where parties and individuals are free to present their ideas to the electorate at regular intervals and politicians are held publicly accountable for their actions. So the Church "values the democratic system" for its ability to involve citizens in the making of political choices, and giving them the opportunity to replace their political leaders by peaceful means *(CA, 46)*. But she warns that authentic democracy requires not only the rule of law, but also "a correct conception of the human person" (along with the rights that go with that conception), and a "balanced hierarchy of values"; for, as history demonstrates, "a democracy without values easily turns into open or thinly disguised totalitarianism" *(CA, 46, 47)*.

That is why the Pope has been so insistent that a country which makes abortion and euthanasia legal has started to dismantle the very basis of its democratic form of government, which means nothing - and quickly becomes a power game - if it is not founded on a real veneration for each and every human person as such. The Church's main contribution to the political order is "precisely her vision of the dignity of the person revealed in all its fulness in the mystery of the Incarnate Word" *(CA, 47)*. Different political systems, different policies, must be judged on the basis of whether or not they serve the true interests of the human person and the common good. Truth cannot be determined by a majority vote.

War and Peace, Crime and Punishment

Whether in the form of warfare or of crime, dealing with violence is one of the main tasks of political authority, which exists in large part to protect the lives and interests of its citizens.

There have always been pacifist Christians, but most have accepted the need, on occasion, to use force in self-defence or the defence of the family. Neither John the Baptist nor Christ explicitly condemned all use of violence or the bearing of arms - the spirit of revenge and retaliation was condemned, and peacemaking commended, but this is not quite the same thing. An individual person may be called to renounce violence altogether, even in extreme circumstances, following the example of Christ himself, but this has to be a free decision of the person; it cannot be imposed by others. As with the renunciation of earthly goods such as property or marriage, pacifism belongs to the state of "extreme normality" that testifies in the midst of the world to a kingdom of peace that exists in the heart of Christ.

What the Church has tried to do, rather than abolish the more violent instincts of the fallen human race, is to channel and moderate them. As Christian civilization emerged in Europe after the conversion of the various barbarians who had engulfed the territories of the old Roman Empire, the eleventh century saw a peace movement called the "Truce of God" which permitted warfare only on ninety days of the year, and sought to guarantee protection for non-combatants such as priests, peasants, pilgrims and women. It was short lived, and the Crusades which followed saw the attempt to channel and even sanctify violence in defence of the Holy Places diverted by less noble ambitions. (The appaling sack of the Christian city of Constantinople by the knights of the Fourth Crusade in 1204 provides a classic example.)

From the time of St Augustine, Catholic thinkers had tried to analyse the conditions for a "just war", and these have been reaffirmed even in the new *Catechism*. They apply only to a war of self-defense by a legitimate political authority, and even then the damage inflicted by the aggressor must have been "lasting, grave, and certain", all other means of putting an end to the conflict must have been "shown to be impractical or ineffective", there must be "serious prospects of success", and the result of resorting to arms "must not produce evils and disorders graver than the evil to be eliminated" *(Catechism, 2309)*. Nor does the Church recognize the concept of "total war": moral rules still apply, and so "non-combatants, wounded soldiers and prisoners must be respected and treated humanely" *(Catechism, 2313)*.

It is unlikely that any of these conditions can be met in the modern world, where the technological power of weaponry has grown beyond the conception of our ancestors. The stockpiling of arms even for purposes of deterrence, and the international trade in such weapons, is similarly questionable. The Church has placed growing emphasis on the need for international arbitration to settle disputes between nations. We are to strive towards peace by working for justice and economic development, so as to prevent material resentments from building up into causes for aggression *(Catechism, 2315-7, 2438)*.

The principle of self-defence also applies within the polity, since it is based on respect for the individual person. Laws which are set by the authorities to regulate life within the State must be consistent with the Natural Law if they are to be truly legitimate (although they need not try to make illegal everything that is immoral). They are designed to facilitate the pursuit of human fulfilment, and those who deliberately break such laws are acting against the common good. Punishment may serve as deterrent for others, as a way of redressing the disorder caused and as a form of expiation for the criminal: it ought never to be an act of revenge; nor does the criminal ever lose his human dignity or his right to humane treatment.

Once again, while the Church has always recognized the State's right to resort to the death penalty, under modern conditions it is deemed that the cases where a criminal could not be securely prevented from committing further crimes - thus necessitating capital punishment - "are very rare, if not practically non-existent" *(Catechism, 2267)*.

Abortion and Euthanasia

We live in a society that grants the legal "right" to the abortion of an unwanted child, which produces thousands of embryos a year for experimentation and then discards them, and which now seems to be moving towards the approval of medical euthanasia or "mercy killing" of human beings. The Pope has called this a *culture of death*.

The exact moment at which the embryo becomes capable of sensation or consciousness will not concern us here. Like arguments about "viability" (or the medieval concept of "animation") it would distract us from the main point, which is that a human life recognizably distinct from its mother begins with the fertilization of an egg. Whether or not it subsequently splits into two lifeforms, *at least one* human life is present. To attack that life is to risk killing an innocent human being. We know, of course, that millions of early embryos are miscarried naturally, or simply fail to implant in the mother's womb. This does not affect the argument at all. Natural deaths occur at every stage of life, and every life ends in death, but there is a big difference between permitting a death to occur as part of the normal biological process, when it cannot be easily prevented, and bringing that death about deliberately by an act of aggression against it.

Many people fail to understand this simple point. It is a matter of Natural Law, but our ability to discern right from wrong was damaged by the consequences of the Fall, and the natural clarity of our minds is easily dimmed. It may seem to us sometimes as though killing a child in the womb - especially if it is not yet easily recognizable as human, or if its chances of survival are already extremely slim - is the lesser of two evils. That is, in fact, a judgement that as human beings we are not qualified to make. The same applies when it is a question of bringing a premature end to the life of someone old and sick, someone who may even have requested death. (Perhaps life has genuinely become intolerable to them, or perhaps they have been persuaded by relatives or doctors to relieve the pressure on others. The Church does not teach that we must keep anyone alive by any means for as long as possible. Extreme medical procedures can be discontinued without committing sin: *see Catechism, 2278.*) Human beings do not have the ability or the right to perform such actions, and if we do perform them we are not only doing an injustice to the other, but destroying our own soul at the same time. Legislation that approves them destroys the moral authority of the state:

"Respect for the human person entails respect for the rights that flow from his dignity as a creature. These rights are prior to society and must be recognized by it. They are the basis of the moral legitimacy of every authority: by flouting them, or refusing to recognize them in its positive legislation, a society undermines its own moral legitimacy. If it does not respect them, authority can rely only on force or violence to obtain obedience from its subjects" *(Catechism, 1930; cf. 2273).*

Now that the memory of the Nazi death-camps has grown faint, and with the continuing advance of medical technology, there is a great danger that the idea of "eugenics" may again become fashionable (if it is not already).

This is the attempt deliberately to engineer a "superior" race by selective breeding, genetic engineering and the elimination of the "unfit". There may be strong commercial incentives for such developments. At the same time, many of those researchers and medical practitioners who are involved in bringing them about may be doing so with the intention of benefiting the humanity and relieving suffering. The teaching of the Church is nevertheless completely opposed to such policies. "Good intentions" need to be seen in the context of the moral order as a whole.

For the same reason, the Church's opposition to a procedure such as abortion, for example, needs to be integrated with an immense respect for the lives and persons of those woman and families who are tempted to resort to it, or are coping with the consequences of having one. That respect must not be restricted to words, but take some tangible form (as it has done where the Church has offered financial or other support to such families). The campaign to end abortion cannot focus on legality alone, but must recognize the need to heal society, support mothers and families, and educate young people more effectively in the art of moral reasoning.

CIVIL SOCIETY

Without a fabric of trust and friendship, and without the moral and intellectual education that takes place in families above all, neither political nor economic society could function for long. This fabric is often called *civil society*.

Civil society emerges out of the family, and out of the relatively informal association of persons in a community of friendship. At a certain point, more formal structures of exchange and ownership (economic structures), and of government and decision-making (political society) will become essential. Civil society is therefore primary, not because it emerges first in time, but because the others depend upon it. Rodger Charles SJ explains the importance of civil society using a very vivid example:

"It was inadequate forms of democracy which made it possible for Lenin, Mussolini and Hitler [he might have added Stalin] to cheat, lie and bully their ways to power ... with deplorable results for their countries and for the world. If democracy is to work it must do so within a framework of the divine revealed and natural laws, and be supported by a truly civil society, that is, with protection for personal rights and liberties which exist independent of and antecedent to political society and provide the only sound basis for the latter. This civil society is one founded on respect for person and family, a morally responsible citizenry knowing its rights and fulfilling its duties, built up though a network of voluntary organizations, social, political and economic, and based on respect for morally responsible freedom" *(Christian Social Witness and Teaching, Vol. 2. p. 25).*

Covenant

Some modern philosophers have tried to explain human society on the basis of a "social contract", but I think it is more in keeping with the Catholic tradition to speak of a "covenant". A covenant is a mutual commitment that creates a unity of persons so close that it amounts to membership of a family. This is what distinguishes it from a legal contract, which may outwardly resemble it. In a contract, each side agrees to do a certain thing, and once those promises are discharged, the contract ceases. When a covenant is made, on the other hand, a *gift of self* is exchanged. In other words, each person places his or her own soul in the other's power. This is a much deeper, more powerful relationship. It is sealed not just with a signature, but with a sacrifice. Marriage is the most obvious and commonplace example, in which vows are entered into that are so binding and so total that two people are said to become one flesh.

We all know something about the Testament or Covenant that God made with Israel, and which gives its name to the Bible. There is in fact not merely *one* covenant described in the Old Testament, but a whole series of them - covenants with Adam, Noah, Abraham, Moses, David, and so on right up to the New Covenant in Christ. They involve a progressive deepening of the relationship between God and man. In the Old Testament, God is described as having "betrothed" himself to Israel *(see e.g. Hosea 2:19)*. In the New Testament, that betrothal was consummated in the Person of Christ, who was in himself a marriage of heaven and earth, man and God, human and divine nature. The *sacraments of initiation* in the Catholic Church (baptism, eucharist, confirmation) are also forms of covenant - or rather, extensions of the same New Covenant between God and his people that makes us into a family capable of saying together the "Our Father".

"One of the key differences between a society based on contract and one built around the idea of covenant *[brit]*, is what holds it together. A social contract is maintained by an *external* force, the monopoly within the state of the justified use of coercive power. [Thus it is a society of individuals seeking their own benefit and entering into conflict with each other.] A covenant, by contrast, is maintained by an *internalized* sense of identity, kinship, loyalty, obligation, responsibility and reciprocity. These promptings cannot always be taken for granted and have to be carefully nurtured and sustained. Hence the centrality, within covenantal associations, of education, ritual, sacred narratives, and collective ceremony.

"A social contract gives rise to the instrumentalities of the state - governments, nations, parties, the use of centralized power and the mediated resolution of conflict. It is the basis of political society. A covenant gives rise to quite different institutions - families, communities, peoples, traditions, and voluntary associations. It is the basis of civil society. This is one way of understanding the difference between man as a *political* animal and man as a *social* animal." *(Jonathan Sacks, Education, Values and Religion, University of St. Andrews, 1996)*

The Guilds

One of the interesting examples of a covenantal-type organization which would come under the heading of "voluntary associations" is the *guild*. This is an association of working people, often united by a certain craft, and designed to provide a framework for the mutual support of its members and their families. In the Middle Ages such guilds, each under the patronage of some popular saint, were an important part of the civil society of cities and villages. They negotiated the quality, price and distribution of many goods, as well as looking after the education, employment and social welfare of the craftsmen who made them. In more recent times, "friendly societies" with their offers of insurance revived echoes of the guild system, as did "credit unions" which enabled the poor to obtain credit denied them by the High Street banks.

FAMILY

The modern world does not understand covenants, and tries to reduce them all to more superficial and temporary forms of agreement. Guilds become mere clubs, societies or trade unions: the latter, especially, very useful and important in their own right, but often concerned more with negotiating better rates of pay than with supporting an entire way of life and social structure. Meanwhile marriage is fast becoming a temporary legal arrangement to facilitate the cohabitation of willing partners. That is because the modern world views human beings as individuals, atomic social "particles", bound together in temporary molecules that can be split apart for the sake of convenience and reassembled whenever necessary - that is, by contract.

The Basis of Marriage

In the face of all of this, the Christian (and especially the Catholic) faith proposes a much more challenging vision, based on an understanding of the Natural Law by which we are made. As we have seen, a person "cannot fully find himself through a sincere gift of self" *(Gaudium et Spes, 24)*. And thus: "Man cannot live without love. He remains a being that is incomprehensible for himself, his life is senseless, if love is not revealed to him, if he does not encounter love, if he does not experience it and make it his own, if he does not participate intimately in it" *(RH, 10)*. The family founded on lasting marriage between a man and a woman is the place where that love is normally first revealed to us, where we encounter it - through a parent's smile, perhaps - and where we go on to make it our own and participate in it.

Remember that "love" here means not primarily the affectionate, romantic or erotic feelings that we may experience at any given moment. These inevitably come and go, and though we take them into account, we cannot live our lives by them without falling into personal and social chaos. Nor, when John Paul II speaks of love as the "fundamental and innate vocation of every human being" *(FC, 11)*, does he simply mean love as an *act of will*. He intends to refer, rather, to a *relationship between persons*: a relationship that involves a commitment of self one to the other, and a sharing of substance in a particularly intense form of "communion".

John Paul II has written and spoken so much on this theme of marriage and self-gift that it may well be called the central theme of his pontificate, and his most distinctive contribution to Catholic thought. In an early series of Wednesday audiences he expounded a theological commentary on the creation of man and woman, and on the importance of the body in spiritual love, which has come to be known as his "theology of the body". Growing out of his own much earlier philosophical researches, as well as his extensive pastoral work with families, this enabled him to deepen the Church's response to the social crisis of the family in our times, and to the many critics of Paul VI's controversial encyclical, *Humanae Vitae* (1968).

Contraception and Covenant

For John Paul II, the condemnation of barrier and chemical forms of birth control by Paul VI was rooted in the Church's long-standing affirmation (against the Manichees and other dualists who believed that the material world was made not by God but by an evil force) of the spiritual value of the human body as an essential dimension of the person, and of the goodness of marriage. Sexuality, "by means of which man and woman give themselves to one another through the acts which are proper and exclusive to spouses, is by no means purely biological, but concerns the innermost being of the human person as such" *(FC, 11)*. Thus a spouse's withholding of the dimension of fertility in any given act of love damages the totality not just of a physical but of a spiritual act. This is why the Church judges that it would be better - if there are good reasons (and there may be) against conceiving a child - to abstain from the act altogether rather than mutilate it. Our "vocation to love" can be expressed either in marriage or in celibacy, but either way the human body is involved in establishing an exclusive relationship of self-gift - whether to one's spouse in the vows of marriage, or directly with God in some form of special reserve or consecration.

This "spousal" relationship is itself an image of the relationship of divine Persons in the Trinity, and it is "trinitarian" in the sense that it is in the nature of such an exclusive communion to be unselfish, and therefore to be open to any new life that may arise from love: the child, for example, who is a gift and a grace flowing from the presence of the Holy Spirit. Thus marriage is inseparable from the *idea of family* - even though many couples are childless for reasons beyond their control, without this affecting the validity or value of their marriage. The couple's hospitality or openness to life extends not only to the engendering and nurturing of children, but also to their education: the Church teaches that parents are the primary educators of their children.

All of this is implicit in Holy Scripture, for (as St Thomas Aquinas among others saw very clearly) the mystical key to understanding the Old Testament is found in the Song of Songs, and the key to the New Testament is found in the Book of Revelation, in the Wedding Feast of the Lamb and the descent of the Bride from heaven *(Rev. 19:6-10, 21:1-4)*. Creation, Trinity, Incarnation and

Redemption: all these mysteries of the faith are bound together, and all express themselves in Covenant and Marriage. Yet the Church never loses sight of the fact that marriage is only capable of becoming a sacrament of the Church because it is first of all *natural*. Even the indissolubility of a validly contracted marriage is part of its natural essence, not some arbitrary dogma imposed upon it, for the power to establish a covenantal union of two lives lies within the mature power of man and woman from the moment of their creation. (On all of this, please read the beautiful *Letter to Families* by John Paul II, which was written for the UN's Year of the Family, 1994.)

ECOLOGY

Pope John Paul II used an unusual metaphor to describe the family founded on marriage in *Centesimus Annus*. He called it "the first and fundamental structure of 'human ecology'" *(CA, 39)*. Of course, the use of the word "ecology" is relatively recent in Catholic Social Teaching, but this use of it is particularly apt, because in the original Greek it refers to the order or "logic" of a household. That is to say, it has to do with housekeeping: with homemaking.

This original meaning is also what lies behind the use of the word to describe one of the newest of the sciences. The science of ecology treats the whole earth as the "home" of humankind, and studies the ordering of this, our natural environment. What it reveals above all - and what makes it so fascinating - is the complex interconnectedness of all living processes on the planet. Since the 1970s (by which time the first photographic images of the earth from space had imprinted themselves on the consciousness of a generation), ecological science has flourished in parallel with the political Green movement, so that by now conservation, biodiversity and greenhouse gas emissions are the common currency of headlines and conferences around the world. So-called "green" concerns are no longer exclusively tied to progressive or socialistic politics, but have become practically universal - although it has to be said there is wide disagreement over the implications of such concerns.

The 'Greening' of Catholicism

Beginning with his first encyclical, *Redemptor Hominis* in 1979 *(see sections 15 and 16 in particular)*, Pope John Paul II worked to establish a response to ecological concerns as an essential element in Catholic Social Teaching. In 1988 *Sollicitudo Rei Socialis* he developed his ideas further, and in the January 1990 *Message for the World Day of Peace* summed up these developments in what became a veritable "manifesto" for Green Catholicism, insisting that the new ecological awareness, "rather than being downplayed, ought to be encouraged to develop into concrete programmes and initiatives." He called for "carefully co-ordinated solutions based on a morally coherent world view." He described the ecological crisis as fundamentally a *moral* issue. For "there is an order in the universe that must be respected, and... the human person endowed with the capability of choosing freely, has a grave responsibility to preserve this order for the well-being of future generations."

These points were reaffirmed in *Centesimus Annus* (sections *37-40*). There and in *Evangelium Vitae* in 1995 *(especially section 42)* he integrated them with his fundamental teaching on the sanctity and defence of human life in the family and the wider society, referring again to "human ecology" and describing man as the being who is "called to till and look after the garden of the world". "Not only has God given the earth to man, who must use it with respect for the original good purpose for which it was given to him, but man too is God's gift to man. He must therefore respect the natural and moral structure with which he has been endowed" *(CA, 38)*. This "Greening of Catholicism" was consolidated, finally, in the *Catechism of the Catholic Church*: for example in the section on "respect for the integrity of creation" *(paras 2415-18)*, which also enjoins kindness to animals, citing the examples of St Francis of Assisi and St Philip Neri (but when did you ever hear of a saint who was *cruel* to animals?). The *Catechism's* commentary on the eight days of creation and resurrection (paras 337-49) is particularly noteworthy for its emphasis on the interdependence and solidarity of all creatures.

Every gesture we make, every breath we take, every mouthful we eat, every sight we see connects us to the entire fabric of creation, on which we depend, and which we affect in our turn. Christianity gives us no excuse to plunder creation, but it does perhaps help to explain the reasons *why* we do. The doctrine of Original Sin describes the beginning of the process - though not the end. It is in Jesus Christ that all things "hold together" *(Col. 1:17)*, and in him they will once again be healed and reintegrated. Not for Christianity the sad, bleak view that, since animals and plants have no immortal souls, they cannot in some way share in the Resurrection. No, the cosmos will be transfigured, eternalized, perfected *in its living integrity*, which includes all that is good in the creatures that currently adorn it. But it will pass through death as through a refining fire, and emerge remoulded in the image and likeness of God in a way we cannot imagine.

A Call for Reform

This vision and these principles are intended by the Pope to guide and inspire our thinking, but not to determine public policy or private initiative in any detail. It is the job of the faithful to work out any practical implications. Nevertheless, in *Centesimus Annus* and here in his *1990 Peace Day Message*, the Pope does spell out some of these:

"The ecological crisis reveals the urgent moral need for a new solidarity, especially in relations between the developing nations and those that are highly industrialized. States must increasingly share responsibility, in complementary ways, for the promotion of a natural and social environment that is both peaceful and healthy... The newly industrialized States cannot, for example, be asked to apply restrictive environmental standards to their emerging industries unless the industrialized States first apply them within their own boundaries. At the same time, countries in the process of industrialization are not morally free to repeat the errors made in the past by others, and recklessly continue to damage the environment through industrial pollutants, radical deforestation or unlimited exploitation of non-renewable resources. In this context, there is urgent need to find a solution to the treatment and disposal of toxic wastes. It must also be said that the proper ecological balance will not be found without directly addressing the structural forms of poverty that exist throughout the world. Rural poverty and unjust land distribution in many countries, for example, have led to subsistence farming and to the exhaustion of the soil. Once their land yields no more, many farmers move on to clear new land, thus accelerating uncontrolled deforestation, or they settle in urban centres which lack the infrastructure to receive them. Likewise, some heavily indebted countries are destroying their natural heritage, at the price of irreparable ecological imbalances, in order to develop new products for export. In the face of such situations it would be wrong to assign responsibility to the poor alone for the negative environmental consequences of their actions. Rather, the poor, to whom the earth is entrusted no less than to others, must be enabled to find a way out of their poverty. This will require a courageous reform of structures, as well as new ways of relating among people and States."

The structural changes the Pope calls for in society (both here and in *Centesimus Annus*) must be accompanied by a profound change in individual lifestyles, especially in the West. As he says, if those changes do not come voluntarily, they will eventually be forced upon us. "Simplicity, moderation and discipline, as well as the spirit of sacrifice, must become a part of everyday life, lest all suffer the negative consequences of the careless habits of a few." A culture of life would have to be a culture not of consumerism but of moderation - and (where necessary) of asceticism.

JUSTICE

We have already seen that the heading under which much of Catholic Social Teaching belongs is traditionally that of "Justice": itself one of the four Cardinal Virtues. It is time that we looked more directly at this concept.

Human Rights

These days it is hard to discuss questions of justice without also using the language of "human rights". It was Pope John XXIII who first began to introduce this phrase into the official teaching of the Church. In the previous century it had been associated mainly with anti-Catholic Liberalism and the Enlightenment - although of course the concept has a much longer Christian (and pre-Christian) history. It is important to understand the modern use and meaning of the term in Catholic teaching, even if it means venturing a little bit further into philosophy, because there is a widespread tendency today to claim anything and everything as a "right", and in so doing to devalue the term altogether.

What is it then, in the Christian understanding, that gives us a genuine "right" to anything at all - to life, education or liberty, for example? And what is the first

or most important of human rights? The Roman
Catholic Bishops of England and Wales, in their document *The Common Good, 1997*, are very clear about
this. They state that, "The study of the evolution of the
idea of human rights shows that they all flow from the
one fundamental right: the right to life. From this
derives the right to those conditions which make life
more truly human: religious liberty, decent work, hous-
ing, health care, freedom of speech, education, and the
right to raise and provide for a family" *(section 37)*.
They also warn: "Not everything said to be a 'right'
really is one. There is no 'right to choose' to harm
another, for instance. The proliferation of alleged
'rights' can devalue the very concept. So can the ampli-
fication of rights without equivalent stress on duties,
and without some sense of the common good to which
all have an obligation to contribute" *(section 36)*.

So what is the link between these ideas, and particularly of rights and duties? If I have a "right" to life, it
must mean that everyone else has a *duty* towards me,
to help preserve my life, or at least not to take it away.
For if others did not have this duty, I would have no
right: it would be an empty word. Rights and duties
must therefore be inseparable. They are inseparable,
also, from the idea of *society*, because they cannot
exist in a vacuum. They belong to a relationship
between persons.

The Road to Happiness

That I have a "right" or "duty" may be a fact; but what kind of fact is it? Obviously it is not just a fact about me like the fact that I have blue eyes or black hair. Nor is it just a fact about my relationships like the fact that I am married to X or the son of Y. It is a *moral* fact; that is to say, it is a fact about such things as what I *ought to do or be allowed to do*, and about the *use I should make of my freedom*.

It is important to note that the European philosophers of the modern period (such as Hume, Hobbes and Bentham) did not really believe in moral facts of this sort. They concluded that morality is to do with what we *want to do*, and what we may happen to *agree* amongst ourselves to do, in order to advance our interests, minimize our pain and maximize our pleasure. This led them eventually to propose an entirely evolutionary and materialist account of it. According to them, there is nothing - "objectively" speaking - that we *must* do, or refrain from doing.

Christian tradition, on the other hand, says that there *are* moral facts (e.g. rights and duties). These are based not on what we ourselves decide, but on the truth about human nature - on what it is, and especially on what its purpose is. In a way, the modern philosophers were right that morality must be based on the search for happiness. But they were wrong in their analysis of where happiness lies. It does not lie merely in having as much physical pleasure as possible before we die. As we have seen, the basis of Christian anthropology is the idea that every human being is a person created *by and for* the God who is love. Our true happiness lies in him, and the way to that happiness is through trying to become holy.

In the Natural Law tradition, justice is to do with the *repayment of debts*. The very word "ought" (as in "I ought to do this") is connected with the word "owe". In the first place I owe a debt to God (for the world and my own existence). I owe a debt to my parents. I owe a debt to society in general. This is all true, but the Christian anthropology tradition goes further than the concept of indebtedness. It deepens our understanding of the Natural Law by reminding us that we are created not only *by* God but *for* God. That is, we are each created with a purpose. God has made me incomplete or unfinished until I become united with him in the Spirit, which I can only do by the exercise of my personal freedom. That is what my freedom is created *for*. That is what Christ died on the Cross to make possible for me.

Moral obligation comes from the fact that I am not just a stone, or a plant, or a thing (or a statistic, or a consumer), but a person with an immortal destiny. I have a purpose, and that means that I have been commissioned by God himself, who sent me into the world, to *do* something. This gives me the right to whatever I need to accomplish that task without compromising the mission of others, and it lays on others the corresponding duty to help me.

According to Christianity, we have a basic right to do what we were created to do: to live, to love, and to seek God. Others have a duty to allow (or help) us to do what we are created to do. We have a duty - which is just as binding - to allow (or help) others to do what *they* are created to do. From this simple fact we may deduce that every person has a right to life, and in addition to this a right to education, to freedom, to worship, to make a family, to own property, to be educated, to receive a just wage (that is, one sufficient to support a family) - and all the other legitimate rights that the Church has defined.

These rights, together with the duties that go with them, flow from our nature as human beings, that is to say, as human persons, rooted in God and called to share the life of God, which is love. But we especially need to respect and protect those who lack the power or the visibility to defend these rights for themselves - the poor, the unborn, the sick, the uneducated, the homeless. As always, the Christian vision should turn everything around: worry first about justice for others, and one's own rights will take care of themselves.

FREEDOM

The question of justice leads naturally to that of freedom. Ever since 1789, when the French revolutionaries first raised high the banners of "Liberty, Equality, Fraternity", liberation has been the great ideal of every political movement. How can there be justice without freedom? For many people, the two ideas have almost become synonymous. But what does "freedom" actually mean?

Two Traditions

For the Natural Law tradition, the most important moral question is *What is it good to be?* There is an emphasis on the moral virtues, which define our character, and on the exercise of personal responsibility by each individual as the expression of a unique personality. As we have just seen, this tradition also teaches that human beings have a *purpose* which is given to them by their nature, and that they can only fulfil themselves and become truly happy by attaining that goal. Freedom according to the Natural Law tradition was empowerment *to be good*, and thus to do the right thing. It was freedom "for" something.

Another tradition - associated with William of Ockham - defines the important moral question differently. Instead of "What is it good to be?" the question becomes *What is it good to do?* The emphasis is therefore on the exercise of the will, rather than on the person whose will is being exercised. Freedom for this second tradition was freedom "from" something (and mainly freedom from constraint). There is no human "nature" that shows what we must do, no pre-given "goal" towards which we must strive; but instead we choose or construct our own goals, action by action. Ockham himself went so far as to say that what makes one action good and another bad is not anything intrinsic to the action itself, but simply whether it accords or not with what God has (arbitrarily) decided to call "good". There is no cosmic Wisdom involved, there are no universal "ideas" that could constrain God in this decision about what is good and evil: he simply *decides*. Ockham's thought thus brought into question the traditional role of philosophy as the mediator between faith and intelligence. Over the succeeding centuries, it may even have helped shape the common assumption that the more choices we have - the more things we can choose to have - the better off we are. This is the assumption that underlies modern consumerist attitudes *(see CA, 36)*: in the end we become defined by what we possess, or even by the very *power to choose*.

In the other, more ancient tradition, which is also the tradition of the virtues, it doesn't matter so much how many choices we have - how much "power to choose" -

the question is whether we possess the interior strength to *do the right thing*. For the Natural Law tradition, a man does not become more free by becoming able to sin. God and the saints in heaven are not *less free* than us: quite the opposite. The artist is not *less free* because he is constrained by the limitations of his medium, whether paint or stone: in fact the limitations of his medium are the very conditions that permit him to be an artist.

The influence of Ockham and his followers was immense and far-reaching. It even helped to undermine the ideas of legal justice and distributive justice, leaving the focus on reciprocal justice alone. For it led to the belief that there are really no persons (in the Christian sense), *only individuals*. A society is a collection of social atoms, held in check by some kind of government purely for the sake of mutual self-protection. Community, society, common good: these words are just fictions. All justice, therefore, can be analysed solely in terms of individual relationships. (These individualistic ideas even affected some thinkers in the Natural Law tradition, so that they too began to neglect the notion of virtue, except as a way of codifying different types of moral action.)

To question all of this is to question one of the most basic assumptions of the modern world. But we have to question it, for the sake of our sanity and the creation of a humane society.

WORK

Shared ideas may be invisible, but they can shape the way a whole society will think and act. They are visible in their effects. We live our lives by an unconscious philosophy of freedom. We also have a philosophy of *work*. What does the Church say about this?

John Paul II's 1981 encyclical *Laborem Exercens* describes work as "the essential key" to the whole social question. The Christian vision of man is one in which our work of "subduing" and "cultivating" the earth (these are biblical expressions from *Genesis 1:28* and *2:15*) is not the result of the Fall or a punishment for sin (although sin made it onerous), but from the very beginning an aspect of the human vocation. Work forms us in the image of God, whose own work of creation - in the six "days" - also implies a continuing care for what he has made, extending even to the redemptive labour of Christ on the Cross.

The Priority of Labour

Work includes every form of action by which the world is transformed and shaped or even simply maintained by human beings. It includes manual labour, agriculture, science, industry and art. In each case, the value of the work, and its true purpose, lies not so much in the work itself but in the human beings who are acting. It is through work that we achieve fulfilment as human beings: we should be able to become "more human" through our work *(LE, 9)*. Of course, quite often we feel the very opposite: we feel that our work *dehumanizes* us. But this is for one of three main reasons:

(1) The particular work we are doing, though perfectly good in itself, may not be what we ourselves feel called to do (the "square peg in a round hole" syndrome). (2) The work may be in some way immoral or degrading in itself: working for an abortion clinic, for example, or making a pornographic movie. (3) The job may also be set up in such a way that we are treated as "less than human" by our firm or colleagues or customers: the goal of the firm might be perfectly fine, but we are reduced to the status of being little more than tools, or "wage slaves", having no stake in what we are doing other than the pay packet at the end of the week.

In these ways, work may be degrading or alienating. It is alienating because it makes us the means rather than the end of the work: it "instrumentalizes" us so that we become someone else's tool. When John Paul II speaks about the "priority of labour over capital", he means that neither the worker nor his labour should be treated as part of the "means of production" owned by those who direct the process *(LE, 7, 12; CA, 41)*. Alienation is the result of exploitation - and this can include the manipulation of opinion and desire by advertisers or the mass media, as much as it includes the various ways in which a worker may be treated badly by his employer.

What is *not* incompatible with human dignity in work is the *gift of self*, which we have already identified as lying at the heart of Catholic Social Teaching. It is in fact often said that the modern world has almost forgotten the idea of "service", in which one person may voluntarily serve another without loss of dignity and freedom. We tend to confuse this with "servility" - allowing ourselves to be used purely for the sake of some anticipated gain, not out of any desire to do good for the other person. But even where paid employment is concerned, the relationship of worker to employer or customer (or in the old days, servant to master) can be transformed by the spirit in which the service is offered and received. Jesus Christ gave us such a model of service when he washed the feet of his disciples.

Something similar applies to private property. A thing can be "mine" in the truest sense only to the extent that it has either been given to me, or is an expression of my own labour and creativity. Of course, we have already seen that there is no absolute right to property in Catholic teaching, because the only true "maker" of all things is God. Even the raw materials we dig out of the ground originally come from him, and we can create nothing without his help. This enables us to define *limits to the market (see CA, 40 and 34)*: "There are goods which by their very nature cannot and must not be bought and sold". This limitation on private ownership applies to common or collective goods necessary to the fulfilment of human life (such as, at the most basic level, light and air and water). But it also applies in a special way to the human body, and the human blood, organs and genetic material that are increasingly offered for sale on the international market. It has been assumed for generations that the enclosing of land, the capturing, taming and husbanding of animals and the cultivation of plants is enough to turn them into "commodities". Now that genetic engineering has led to the patenting of animals and plants, we have to decide how far this assumption can be extended.

Consumerism

The ethical dilemmas connected with work are extremely subtle - one might say spiritual - and yet it is at this subtle level that the tone and quality of a culture, the moral texture of a civilization, is inevitably determined. Will our civilization model itself on the love between the Madonna and Child, or on some other image of human purpose and relationship? The terrible danger that faces us today is that our relationships, including our relationships at work, are being reduced by the prevailing materialism to something mechanical rather than truly interpersonal.

In a consumerist society, we work in order to earn the money we need to purchase and consume material goods. In a society informed by Catholic Social Teaching it would be equally true to say that we *consume in order to work*, because work is one of the ways we fulfil ourselves in the world. The division of labour and the development of much modern technology since the Industrial Revolution involves a loss of that sense of responsibility which the Pope seeks to restore by making the worker a "part-owner of the great workbench at which he is working with everyone else" *(LE, 14)*.

We have almost succeeded in eliminating the old class and caste divisions, in which one whole sector of society was instrumentalized by another, but we seem to have substituted for this another system which instrumentalizes the individual. We collude with this system by refusing to challenge its assumptions in our daily life.

THE COMMANDMENTS

Most people can't remember more than two or three of them, and we tend to see them as increasingly irrelevant in the modern world. I suppose most of us grow up thinking of the Ten Commandments simply as a list of "dos and don'ts", imposed almost arbitrarily by the Old Testament God on the Jewish people. In fact they are much more than that. They reflect the basic structure of the Natural Law insofar as it applies to human society. The new *Catechism* defines them as "immutable" *(para. 2072)*, and uses them in Part Three as the organizing principle for its account of Catholic Social Teaching. For that reason they can help us to sum up everything that has been said so far in this book.

Why should God reveal, and in such a dramatic fashion (amidst the smoke and thunder of *Exodus 19:18*) the very Law he had already written into human hearts? The answer given by the Christian tradition is that the heart of man had grown cold, and was covered over with the effects of so many sins that little light was visible within. In revealing his Law, God was beginning to reveal himself, and indeed to clothe himself in the language and culture of a people prior to taking flesh among them and

Exploring the Ten Commandments

The People of God are constituted by a Covenant with God, and the Commandments (Exodus 20:2-17 and Deuteronomy 5:6-21) give the rules for living within this Covenant, based on the wisdom of God and the principles of Natural Law. They are summed up in the "Two Commandments" of Mt 22:37-9 (based on Dt 6:5, Lv 19:18), as follows:

I. Love the Lord your God with all your heart, and with all your soul, and with all your mind...

1. I am the Lord your God: you shall not
have other gods before me.
2. You shall not take the Name of the Lord
your God in vain.
3. Remember to keep holy the Lord's Day.

II. ...and love your neighbour as yourself

4. Honour your father and mother that,
your days may be long in the land.
5. You shall not kill [i.e murder].
6. You shall not commit adultery.
7. You shall not steal.
8. You shall not bear false witness against
your neighbour.
9. You shall not covet your neighbour's wife.
10. You shall not covet your neighbour's goods.

The *Ten Commandments* are summarized in the *Two Great Commandments*. But the Two Great Commandments, in turn, are summarized by Jesus in what he calls the **New Commandment**: "Love one another, *as I have loved you*" *(John 13: 34, 15:9-17).*

becoming man. The Old Testament is in continuity with the New, and the Ten Commandments are taken up again by Christians, being read by them in the Spirit they have received from Christ.

The Meaning of the Commandments

The Commandments were intended to establish a special relationship between God and the people of Israel: the "Mosaic Covenant". This relationship is a *family* relationship. God becomes the "Father" of this people in a very special sense. He also becomes their King. The Ten Commandments may thus be seen as the basis for an entire civilization, in each of its essential dimensions

In 1998, Pope John Paul II issued an Apostolic Letter called *Dies Domini*, "*On Keeping the Lord's Day Holy*". In this Letter he explored the meaning of the Commandments insofar as it is applicable not just to the Jewish civilization but to all of human society. Section 13 refers to the Decalogue as ten "words" which represent "the very pillars of the moral life inscribed on the human heart", and the "basic structure of ethics". The first three, he said, are the foundation for everything that follows: for the structural rules governing human community. Without religion, without worship of the divine principle, the only possible result is an ever-greater tendency to close in upon the self, until finally it is "every man for himself". We do have to "look out for Number One": but the true "Number

One" is not myself; it is my Creator. By putting God first -
in the first three Commandments - what we are doing is
re-centering the self. In fact, worship (assuming that it is
worship of that which deserves to be worshipped!) is the
only way that the human self can be turned "inside out"
and begin to become "unselfish". Love starts with this
ability to turn outwards, this awakening to the Other.

The third Commandment - the keeping holy of one
day in seven, its consecration as a special day of worship, rest and celebration - establishes a "great school
of charity, justice and peace" and gives us the "inspira-
tion to change the structures of sin in which individuals, communities and at times entire peoples are entan-
gled" *(section 73)*. It issues from the first two and pre-
pares us for all that follows - all that makes up the
human society which flourishes after the "Seventh
Day" when God had completed his own work and wait-
ed for man's response. The Seventh Day is the beginning and end of the human world. It is the Day in which
human history unfolds, and it is the Rest of God into
which all will be gathered again at the end, when man
too is able to have peace at last.

Earlier on the Cardinal Virtues were described as
something like the foundations of a building. If so, the
Commandments provide the structure of the building that
is set upon those foundations. The roof which shelters
and protects the building and holds it together against the

wild elements outside is *religion*, and this is described in the **first three Commandments**: love God before all else, worship him, and build your society around him. The **other seven Commandments** are like the pillars and walls that support the roof. You cannot truly be said to love the God you cannot see if you fail to love the neighbour that you can see: as Our Lord was to say, you have to love that neighbour as yourself. You have to serve the common good of all. The seven Commandments of the love of man describe the different ways in which we must serve the common good - that is, if we are to live together in harmony, to mutual benefit.

Of these, **the fourth Commandment** is like the central pillar (the hearth? the doorway?) of the building. It is the respect we give to our parents, and to our tradition or our people. This is what preserves the "land", the nation, to which we belong. This is also the way we enter the building and dwell in it: we enter the house from within, we are born and grow up within it. John Paul II has a commentary on this Commandment in his *Letter to Families (section 15)*: "The fourth Commandment of the Decalogue deals with the family and its interior unity - its solidarity, we could say.... In order to bring out the communion between generations, the *divine legislator could find no more appropriate word than this*: 'Honour...' *(Ex. 20:12)*... The family is a community of particularly intense interpersonal relationships: between spouses, between parents and children, between generations. It is a community which must be safeguarded in a special way. And God cannot find a better safeguard than this: 'Honour'."

Commandments **five and six** describe the sacredness of life and marriage; **seven and eight** describe the sacredness of property and truth. Commandments **nine and ten** reinforce the preceding four by emphasizing the need to be *content with what you have*: in other words, they tell us to keep our own desires under control, so that envy and greed and resentment do not spring up like weeds in the house and destroy it. These commandments allude to the *mystery of purity*, much neglected in our semi-pornographic culture but vital in the spiritual life. What happens in our imagination is an intrinsic part of who we are: we should do what we can to protect innocence and modesty.

In other words, taken all together, the last six Commandments develop the implications and fill in the details of what it means to give worship to God and honour to the source of the family - to our own progenitors in God. Jesus Christ, being both God and man, unites the two sets of Commandments in his own Person: the three Commandments of the love of God, and the seven of the love of man. He is at one and the same time the God we must love with all our heart and soul and mind, and the neighbour we must love as ourselves.

From Commandments to Beatitudes

The Gospel writers were very conscious of the fact that Christ, as well as being the Son of God, was the successor to Moses, and the bringer of a new Law as well as a New Covenant. Almost certainly, they had this in mind when describing what came to be called the Sermon on the Mount. Just as Moses taught the Law from a mountain where he came face-to-face with God, so Jesus (who was himself the face of God) taught the new Law from a "mountain" in Galilee.

The coming of Christ did not mean that the Law of Moses had been abrogated, merely that it had been fulfilled and transfigured *(Catechism, 1968)*. The Law of Moses was itself a liberating thing, not a terrible burden from which the Jews needed to be set free (though they did need to be freed from the legalistic minds that failed to understand the spirit of the Law). This was all in the mind of John Paul II when he wrote as follows:

"Man's relationship with God is not one of fear, of slavery or oppression; rather, it is a relationship of serene trust born of a free choice motivated by love. The love which God expects from his people is their response to that faithful and solicitous love which he first made known in all the various stages of salvation history.

"For this very reason the *Commandments*, before being a legal code and a set of juridic regulations, were understood by the chosen people *as an event of grace*, as a sign of their being privileged to belong to the Lord. It is significant that Israel never speaks of the Law as a burden, but rather as a gift and a grace: 'Happy are we, O Israel,' exclaims the prophet, 'for we know what is pleasing to God' *(Bar. 4:4)*.

"The people knew that the Decalogue involves a binding commitment, but they also knew that it is *the condition for life*: Behold, says the Lord, I am setting before you life and death, good and evil; and I command you to observe my commands, *that you may have life (cf. Dt 30:15)*. By his Law God does not intend to coerce man's will, but rather to set it free from everything that could compromise its authentic dignity and its full realization." (John Paul II to government leaders, 5 November 2000.)

The Ten Commandments are the rules by which we are made. If it were not for them, we would not exist. They are revealed in this particular form in order to reorient or redirect us to our true end. The order of the Commandments corresponds to the necessary order of this reorientation, the order of charity. The New Law of the Sermon on the Mount reveals the *pattern of beatitude*, the goal of human nature implicit in the Commandments, which is also the form of holiness. This crowns the Commandments and reveals the fulfilment for which they exist.

The Sermon on the Mount has been called a "self-portrait" of Jesus, in the sense that the pattern of holiness which it gives us is exemplified primarily in Jesus himself. Jesus himself is the Meek One, the Pure of Heart, the One who Mourns over Israel, the One who Hungers and

Thirsts for Righteousness, and so on. Most preachers are in some degree hypocritical. They do not practice what they preach. Jesus is the exception. As the Incarnate Son of God, Jesus is the Law incarnate. He is in his own Person the goal of human existence.

Theologians say that grace does not supplant or destroy the natural order, but rather integrates and assumes it. In the case of the natural law codified in the Commandments we can see this very well. Jesus brings a supernatural fulfilment of our natural yearnings for life and friendship and community and peace. Those yearnings are reflected in the Decalogue but cannot be satisfied except in the life which is described in the Beatitudes. That life, which is both divine and human, natural and supernatural, is opened to us through the *sacraments* that implant within us a receptivity adequate to the infinity of the gift.

CONCLUSION: LIVING IN CHRIST

Until now, I have said very little about the sacraments, and yet it is only with their help that Catholics hope to live the teaching of the Church. "Being a true Christian" is not the same as merely holding a set of beliefs about good and evil behaviour, just and unjust action, and then trying to live up to these standards by our own strength, or forcing others to do so through legislation and political pressure. Unless we receive some kind of divine assistance, the task is impossible.

"I find it to be a law that when I want to do right, evil lies close at hand. For I delight in the law of God, in my inmost self, but I see in my members another law at war with the law of my mind and making me captive to the law of sin which dwells in my members. Wretched man that I am! Who will deliver me from this body of death?" *(Rom. 7:21-24)*. For St Paul, the question is a rhetorical one: the answer is Jesus. "For the law of the Spirit of life in Christ Jesus has set me free from the law of sin and death" *(Rom. 8:2)*.

We have been "set free", and yet if we look at the behaviour of Christians, or the history of Christendom, there seems very little evidence of this freedom. In the words of G.K. Chesterton, "Christianity has not been tried and found wanting; it has been found difficult and left untried." Our perspective changes only when we look at the saints. The saints are those who have begun to put Christianity into practice. Far from being exotic or remote figures with their heads in the clouds, they have always been found in the hurly-burly of everyday life, getting to grips with the real world. In fact, the Church tells us that each of us can and should become a saint ourselves. There is no other way to discover or become our "true selves". We have seen already that Christianity has an enormous respect for the human person in all its uniqueness. This is just another application of the same principle. There is a particular sanctity for each person: instead of making us blend in with all the other "good people", the struggle to become holy makes us more different, more unique, more ourselves, than we would be by staying as we are.

What makes saints possible is prayer and the sacraments, which unite us with Christ. The Church is an extension of the Incarnation. We live in Christ through belonging to the Church; that is, through participating in the sacraments. By joining ourselves together in the Spirit of Christ which is given through the sacraments, we allow God to incarnate himself within our own lives. This is the only way the Creator can complete his work in creatures that he has made to be free. Holiness

- or spiritual beauty - depends on our voluntary cooperation with his will.

The Lord's Prayer

The *Catechism of the Catholic Church* ends with a
beautiful section (Part Four) called "Christian Prayer".
It is organized around the *Our Father*, which it calls a
"summary" of the whole Gospel. This was the prayer
that Our Lord taught the disciples when they asked him
how to pray. It is "the most perfect of prayers"
(Catechism, 2763), its seven "petitions" expressing all
the dimensions of the heart's longing, which only God
can satisfy: "The Sermon on the Mount is teaching for
life, the Our Father is a prayer; but in both the one and
the other the Spirit of the Lord gives new form to our
desires, those inner movements that animate our lives.
Jesus teaches us this new life by his words; he teaches
us to ask for it by our prayer. The rightness of our life in
him will depend on the rightness of our prayer"
(Catechism, 2764).

We are told in the Sermon on the Mount that the
Kingdom belongs to the needy, the poor. The virtues that
are the treasures of holiness are given only to those who
are receptive to them, not to those who are fat and full
and contented. People who are conscious of their complete dependence on God are living the Lord's Prayer,
asking at all times for their daily bread.

There seems no better way of bringing this book to an end than by reminding ourselves that the Christian life and the struggle for justice is founded on prayer: a prayer which God will answer.

"The Spirit and the Bride say, 'Come.' And let him who hears say, 'Come.' And let him who is thirsty come, let him who desires take the water of life without price" *(Rev. 22:17).*

SUMMARY OF TEACHING DOCUMENTS

Pope Leo XIII, 'Rerum Novarum', 1891
On the Condition of the Working Classes
or The Worker's Charter

The great social problem of our time is the misery of the working classes (the poor) who, no longer protected by the Guilds, are oppressed by the yoke laid on them by a rich minority *(6)*.

The Socialist remedy to this problem is to abolish private property, but this would be unjust, because ownership is a universal right. It would in any case make things worse, because what primarily motivates men to work diligently is the intention of providing for themselves and their families *(7-18, 65-6)*.

The family (the society of the household) is older than the State, and has inviolable rights and duties of its own prior to those of civil society. For example, the father must provide security for his children by transmitting fruitful goods to them by inheritance. The State for its part should aid families in distress, and may act to protect the mutual rights of each family member when these are being violated, but must otherwise respect the family's right to privacy and self-management *(19-21)*.

Inequality and hardship are inevitable (and so the promise of utopia a lie). But Labour and Capital have complementary roles and are not naturally at war. They have duties to one another: employers are obliged in justice not to treat workers as slaves, to allow them opportunities to worship, not to burden women and children with inappropriate work, to pay a just wage *(31-2, 58-60)*. A just wage is a living wage *(61-5)*.

Christian charity goes beyond mere justice, and the rich are exhorted to give alms to help the poor once they have taken care of their own needs *(36)*. Only a return to Christian life and institutions will heal our society. The Church trains humanity in virtue, as well as itself providing for the poor. *(42-3)*.

The State is bound to serve the common interest, in particular by improving the condition of workers and maintaining distributive justice *(48-51)*. Indeed the poor and weak are in greater need of its protection and foresight *(54)*. Revolutionary violence and strikes are great evils, that the State should help to prevent by removing the causes of conflict *(55-6)*.

But the responsibility to avoid conflict is not entirely on the State. Employers and workers themselves can accomplish a great deal. The development of Trades Unions and other associations for mutual aid, especially of workers (somewhat like the old guilds), with or without the involvement of employers, may play a particularly important part *(68-79)*.

Pope Pius XI, 'Quadragesimo Anno', 1931
On Reconstructing the Social Order

Rerum Novarum is the "Magna Carta" of Christian activi-
ty in social matters. It effect was to help "imbue the
minds of workingmen with the Christian spirit" and
awaken "a sense of their true dignity", as well as over-
throwing those "tottering tenets" of Liberalism that previ-
ously hampered the State from intervention on behalf of
workers. Trades Unions have flourished since 1891 (associations of employers are regrettably less common).
Catholic workers may join "neutral" unions if there is no
danger for religion in them - developing their own religious and moral education alongside.

The right to property has both a social and a private
character, and the dangers both of *Individualism* and of
Collectivism must be avoided. The right to property
must also be distinguished from its *use*. Profits (the
fruits of production and of work) do not belong exclusively to the employer or to the employed. A wage contract should be modified where possible by a contract of
partnership, so that wage-earners can share in ownership, management and profit.

A just wage (the level of which to be determined by
negotiation) must also be a family wage. Higher wages
may be paid in view of increased family burdens.
Mothers must not be forced out to work, neglecting
homes and children.

The properly organic form of social life requires that "a larger and higher organization" must never "arrogate to itself functions which can be performed efficiently by smaller and lower bodies" [subsidiarity].

Labour "cannot be bought and sold like any piece of merchandise". The proper ordering of economic affairs "cannot be left to free competition alone", but should be subject to a moral, judicial and social order defended by the State. In this context, industrial relations should be cooperative not adversarial. Big unions ("syndicates") can sometimes become too bureaucratic and political.

Since Pope Leo's day, power has been concentrated in the hands not just of the *owners*, but of "trustees and directors of invested funds". Individualism increasingly sets the tone: "Free competition is dead; economic dictatorship has taken its place". Socialism has evolved into violent Communism on the one hand, and into a milder Socialism on the other that almost resembles Christian social thought. But this is an illusion: "no one can be at the same time a sincere Catholic and a true Socialist", because Socialism is ignorant of the "sublime end both of individuals and of society". *Christian Socialism is a "contradiction in terms."* The parent of Socialism was Liberalism, and its offspring is Bolshevism.[1]

---

[1]. Note that here the Pope is condemning materialistic forms of Socialism. For those who have tried to define Socialism differently, it is arguable whether the same absolute strictures apply. But see *CA*.

Renewal of the Christian spirit is needed especially in view of the growing evils of business and industry world-wide. Our society has fallen from rationalism almost into paganism: "dead matter leaves the factory ennobled and transformed, where men are corrupted and degraded". The Bishops must find and train *lay apostles,* and form Christian study-circles and associations into true "Schools of the Spirit".

John XXIII, *'Mater et Magistra',* 1961
New Light on Social Problems

The Pope summarizes the previous social encyclicals, and picks up on Pius XII's point *(in a broadcast of 1941)* that the right to sustenance takes priority over the right to private property *(43).* Work is both a right and a duty, to be protected by the State.

Global economic development has resulted in grave disparity between rich and poor. True prosperity lies not in wealth but in the equitable distribution of wealth and in the fostering of human dignity. Need for international cooperation *(68-81).*

Workers should own shares. Craft-workers, family farms and cooperative enterprises should be supported by the State with training, taxation, credit and social security *(85-90).* In larger firms, too, the company must be seen as a "community of persons" engaged in a common enter-prise, and workers encouraged to take more responsibility, through education and involvement in political decision-making and international organizations *(91-103)*.

Increasingly, people are valuing wages, and the security that comes from insurance or welfare, over the possession of property. But "the exercise of freedom finds its guarantee and incentive in the right of ownership", provided such ownership is *widely distributed* through all classes of people. Public ownership, however, must be restricted by the principle of subsidiarity. Importance of charity reaffirmed *(104-121)*.

Industrialization results in the growth of cities and the decline of agriculture. Governments must compensate by investing more in public services, and allowing special terms for taxation, credit, insurance and price protection, all to benefit farmers. The family-owned farm is the ideal. Farming has a special dignity. Need for mutual solidarity among farmers, and a political voice *(122-149)*.

Economic aid must not be used as a tool of world domination, a new kind of colonialism. Nor must the pursuit of material well-being lead to the neglect of spiritual values *(157-177)*. The poverty of underdeveloped nations is not to be blamed simplistically on overpopulation: the true picture is more complex and uncertain, and the resources of nature cultivated by human intelligence are "well-nigh inexhaustible". Any population policy must respect human dignity and the laws of life *(185-199)*. Nations dependent on each other live in mutual fear and suspicion (arms race, etc.). The development of mutual trust and the integration of scientific advances in service of the common good depends on the recognition of God's moral order *(200-211)*.

Catholic social teaching is opposed both to materialistic ideologies and to the spirit of hedonism. It is based on the truth of human nature, and must be widely studied and taught, especially by the laity *(212-235)*. This knowledge should not remain abstract and theoretical. *Look - Judge - Act*, within a framework of mutual respect and loyalty to the Church *(236-241)*. Spiritual values take priority over material ones (importance of Sunday worship, etc.). The task of the Church is to humanize and Christianize modern civilization *(242-257)*.

John XXIII, 'Pacem in Terris', 1963
Peace on Earth

This was the first encyclical addressed not only to Catholics but to "all men of goodwill". It calls for a world-wide community of nations founded on common interests and the moral and social laws of human nature *(1-7)*.

Each man is a person with intelligence and free will, rights and duties - for example, rights to life, respect, freedom, truth and education, the right to worship God and choose a state of life, the right to work and own property, to form associations, to emigrate and to participate in public life *(8-27)*.

For each right there is a corresponding duty. Both rights and duties must be recognized and accepted. True freedom lies in accepting responsibility for one's actions. Human society is founded on truth, and the first truth is God himself *(28-45)*.

The authority of the State derives from God; laws contrary to the moral order need not be obeyed. The State's purpose is to serve the common good, by promoting, coordinating and defending the whole range of human rights *(46-62)*.

The State must promote social as well as economic progress: i.e. progress in essential services, insurance, employment, access to culture, etc. *(63-66)*. The Church recommends the division of legislative, administrative and judicial functions, and a written constitution incorporating a charter of human rights *(67-79)*.

Nations as well as individuals are the subjects of rights and duties. Relations between them should be based on the principles of truth, justice and freedom. Racial and cultural minorities must always be treated with respect. Refugees do not lose their rights. Where possible work must be brought to people where they traditionally live, rather than expecting them to move *(80-108)*. Justice, right reason and human dignity cry out against the arms race. In the atomic age, war is no longer a fit instrument to repair the violation of justice *(109-129)*.

Progress in science and technology has led to increased interdependence of all peoples. There must be a common authority, one not imposed by force and which respects the principle of subsidiarity, to safeguard the common good of all. The United Nations Organization, founded 1945, is a step in the right direction *(130-145)*.

We need an educated and active laity. Catholics may and should collaborate with non-Christians and followers of false philosophies in pursuit of practical objectives, provided they are always guided by prudence and the other virtues *(146-172)*.

Peace "is but an empty word, if it does not rest upon that order which Our hope prevailed upon Us to set forth in broad outline in the encyclical. It is an order that is founded on truth, built up on justice, nurtured and animated by charity, and brought into effect under the auspices of freedom" *(167)*.

John Paul II, 'Laborem Exercens', 1981
On Human Work

New technological and social developments are changing the world of work. The focus of Catholic Social Teaching has shifted from questions of labour and class to the global dimension of justice and peace. But work remains the essential key to the social question, which is the question of "making life more human" *(sections 1-3)*. (A detailed spirituality of work is developed in *sections 24-27* of the encyclical.)

Work is defined as something that only man can do, for he has been placed here "in order to subdue the earth" *(cf. Gen. 1:28)*. His work bears "the mark of a person operating within a community of persons". He "reflects the very action of the Creator of the universe" by carrying out his mandate to "subdue" the earth through work, but remains at all times "within the Creator's original ordering" and in his image, both male and female *(4)*.

To "subdue" is to cultivate and transform the visible world (by agriculture, industry, art, science, etc.). In this task, technology is an ally, but can also displace or enslave man, who should always be the "subject" of work *(5)*, working for the sake of his own self-fulfilment. The dignity of labour lies not in the work but in the worker *(6)*. This is known as the "Gospel of work".

Toil and suffering accompanies human work after the Fall (and in some social systems has been used to oppress or degrade), but it is still a good thing, by which man "becomes more a human being". Therefore industriousness is a virtue *(9)*. Work is also an important foundation for family life (the family is the first "school of work") and for the common good of a nation *(10)*.

The modern period was marked by a conflict between labour and capital, or rather between workers and the entrepreneurs who were exploiting them unjustly *(11)*. Marxist ideology sought to bring about a dictatorship of the proletariat, and to eliminate private ownership of the means of production. The Church supports the right to private property: man receives natural resources as a gift from the Creator, and in order to make them bear fruit must take them over "by making them his workbench" *(12)*. But this right is not absolute; it is subordinated to the right to common use *(14)*. "Rigid" capitalism is unacceptable: the means of production should serve labour, if necessary by being socialized through intermediate bodies, or even some form of joint ownership, provided this means that "each person is fully entitled to consider himself a part-owner of the great workbench at which he is working with everyone else", and has a real sense that he is working "for himself" *(15)*.

The Church thus opposes the error of "materialistic economism" *(13)*, against which various movements of solidarity among workers have arisen and should arise: work is not a merchandise to sell to an employer; employees do not constitute a "work force"; man is not merely a "means of production"*(7)*. The Church must defend the worker who is undervalued, underpaid or even unemployed *(8)*. She rejects the separation of labour and capital because both involve "living, actual people" who cannot be reduced to an impersonal force *(14)*.

Work is a moral obligation and therefore connected with various rights, including the right to work or alternatively to unemployment benefits *(16-18)* and to just remuneration *(19)* - e.g. a "family wage" or other measures must preserve the mother's freedom to devote herself to her children and their education - cheap health care, rest, pension, insurance, etc. *(19)*. There is also a right to form unions in order to secure these rights "within the framework of the common good" *(20)*. All of this applies equally to the disabled *(22)* and the immigrant worker *(23)*. Special attention should be given to restoring agricultural work as "the basis for a healthy economy" *(21)*.

John Paul II, *'Centesimus Annus',* 1991, *On 100 years after Rerum Novarum*

John Paul II's major social encyclical begins by paying tribute to Leo XIII, who faced the social problems generated by a new form of property (capital) and a new form of labour (simply for wages). Work is part of the human vocation, but when labour becomes a *commodity to sell*, new injustices can and did arise. In *Rerum Novarum*, Pope Leo defended the essential dignity and rights of workers, together with the principle of solidarity (under its classical name "friendship"). Criticizing both socialism and liberalism, he stated that "the defenceless and the poor have a claim to special consideration".

After sketching the history of the last 100 years - including two world wars, the consolidation of Communist dictatorship, the arms race and the Cold War (complicated outside Europe by decolonization) - John Paul refers to three types of response to the Communist threat: (i) the European social market economies tried to end the situations of injustice that fuelled revolutionary movements by building a "democratic society inspired by social justice"; (ii) others set up repressive systems of national security, which risked destroying the very freedoms they were intended to protect; (iii) while affluent Western societies tried (successfully) to compete with Marxism at its own level, by demonstrating a superior ability to meet human material needs.

With this the Pope comes to "The Year 1989", and his analysis of the Fall of Communism, which he traces to the recovery and application of the principles of Catholic social teaching by Polish workers in the name of solidarity, faced with the inefficiency of the economic system and the spiritual and cultural void brought about by Communism. The consequences of 1989 apply to the Third World, in that they enable the Church to affirm "an authentic theology of integral human liberation" (26), and to Europe, where a great effort is now needed "to rebuild morally and economically the countries which have abandoned Communism". Disarmament should make possible a greater "mobilization of resources" for "economic growth and common development", both in Europe and in the Third World. But development is threatened by resurgent totalitarianism, materialism and religious fundamentalism.

The fourth chapter, on private property and the universal "destination" (purpose) of material goods, is the heart of the encyclical. An individual right to property exists but is limited by nature: it is created by human work, and since the earth as a whole was given to man in common, all possession should be subordinated to the common good. These days, the possession of "know-how, technology and skill" are just as important as material resources in the creation of wealth. This leads to new types of exclusion and poverty, especially in the Third World. To an unjust economic system where fundamental human needs remain unsatisfied and development impossible, one must oppose not socialism but a "society of free work, of enterprise and of participation", in which "the market is appropriately controlled by the forces of society and by the State". In such a system, profit is not the only regulator of the life of business, monopolies are broken down and unpayable debts deferred or cancelled, and every effort is made to create conditions under which the poorer nations may share in development *(35)*.

In advanced economies, the need for basic goods is replaced by the "demand for quality", leading to the danger of *consumerism*: lifestyles directed not towards "truth, beauty, goodness and communion with others for the sake of common growth" but towards acquisition for the sake of "enjoyment as an end in itself", where the definition of human needs has been distorted by a false anthropology. Consumerism *alienates* man from his true self, which can only be attained by self-transcendence and self-gift. It leads to the disordered consumption of natural resources and irresponsible destruction of the environment and the creation of "structures of sin" that impede human development (to which the Pope opposes the structures of "human ecology", starting with the family as sanctuary of life).

Despite its advantages, the market has limits. There are "collective and qualitative needs which cannot be satisfied by market mechanisms" and human goods which must not be bought and sold, but need to be defended by the State and society *(40)*. Marxism has failed, but marginalization, exploitation and alienation persist. The Church endorses the "free economy", but only if economic freedom is "circumscribed within a strong juridical framework which places it at the service of human freedom in its totality", which is ethical and religious at its core *(42)*. She offers her social teaching, however, not as a model but as an "indispensable and ideal orientation" towards the common good.

Human freedom depends on the recognition of an ultimate truth, without which "the force of power takes over", and democracy slides into totalitarianism *(44-5)*. Human rights, starting with the right to life and culminating in religious freedom, must be protected, and the security of stable currency and efficient public services assured, by the State. Families and other intermediate communities and "networks of solidarity" on which the culture of a nation depends should be supported. However, the principle of subsidiarity militates against excessive State interference and control, as occurs in the "Social Assistance State".

The Church contributes to "a true culture of peace" by promoting the truth about human destiny, creation and Redemption, and about our shared responsibility for avoiding war. Peace is promoted by development, which in turn depends on "adequate interventions on the international level" and "important changes in established life-styles", especially in the more developed economies *(51-2, 58)*. The Church's social doctrine is inspired by her care for each human being, and forms a part of her evangelizing and salvific mission, *revealing man to himself* in the light of Christ. Though primarily theological, it is interdisciplinary, and rather than being merely a theory is a basis for action. With the help of grace, "Love for others, and in the first place love for the poor, in whom the Church sees Christ himself, is made concrete in the *promotion of justice" (58)*.

[This precis is reprinted by kind permission of the Catholic University of America Press, from the forthcoming new edition of *The New Catholic Encyclopedia*.]

Bishops of England and Wales, *'The Common Good'*, 1996

In October 1996, with an eye to the forthcoming General Election, the Bishops of England and Wales released *The Common Good and Catholic Social Teaching* (13,000 words), plus detailed notes on the use of the document in study groups. A brief revised summary was produced in 2001 (see Bibliography).

According to this document, the first principle and focal point of the Catholic social vision is the dignity of the human person. God became flesh as a human being, and Christ challenges us to see and serve him in our neighbour, "especially the neighbour who lacks what is essential to human flourishing" (there is a "preferential option for the poor"). Catholic Social Teaching develops through history, and now embraces *democracy* and universal *human rights*, while emphasizing the dependence of both on a system of common values. Observance of the Church's social teaching is not "optional"; it is part of her moral teaching in general, based both on natural law and Revelation. Social and political liberation are an aspect of evangelization.

"God is a divine society of three Persons", and our social nature is an aspect of the divine image in us. Human society can be structured either to facilitate or to frustrate personal development. A well-constructed society will give priority to family life, and will integrate the "vertical" principle of *subsidiarity* with the "horizontal" principle of *solidarity*. The former favours the dispersal of authority "as close to the grass roots as good government allows"; the latter stresses interdependence and common responsibility. These principles must be applied to Britain's relations with the European Union and participation in the international economic order (overseas aid, resolution of debt crisis, restriction of arms sales, encouragement of the poorer economies through regulation of the market). There must also be a "religious respect" for the integrity of creation and the "environmental common goods" which belong to all humanity, present and future.

The common good cannot exclude any section of the population: for example by poverty, even relative poverty. Governments must "arbitrate between the sometimes conflicting demands of a market economy and the common good". While the "centrally commanded economies" have shown themselves to be oppressive, inefficient, wasteful and unresponsive to human needs, the Church also "rejects belief in the automatic beneficence of market forces", which are "just as likely to lead to evil results" (to create an alienated "underclass", to encourage selfishness rather than service, to foster consumerism, etc.) unless "regulated in the name of the common good" within an ethical and legal framework. Social services "need other incentives than mere profit". The free market has undermined a sense of moral responsibility in the *mass media*. In the *world of work*, employment is more than a purely commercial contact, and the worker's rights are superior to those of capital. The Church encourages partnership in business, membership in trade unions and a just minimum wage.

Politics is not an ignoble profession, despite the prevailing climate of suspicion and contempt among and towards politicians. Candidates in an election should be chosen for their general character and attitude, since they will have to represent the electorate in varied and unpredictable circumstances, not on the basis of a single issue such as abortion. It is true, however, that Britain has become a "culture of death", and Catholics must try to awaken the conscience of the majority against "the use or disposal of human life, as a means to another end". The Bishops discern a "national mood of pessimism"; a "weakening of the sense of mutual responsibility and a decline in the spirit of solidarity", thanks to the "growing priority of technology over ethics", "things over persons" and "matter over spirit". "For these threats to be resisted, the political arena has to be reclaimed in the name of the common good."

[This precis is reprinted by kind permission of the Catholic University of America Press, from the forthcoming new edition of *The New Catholic Encyclopedia*.]

BIBLIOGRAPHY

The relevant **papal encyclicals** and other documents of the
teaching authorityare referred to throughout this book, and
many of them are summarized. The encyclicals are available
from the Catholic Truth Society in London, and are also available on the Web (see below). The abbreviations used in the text
are as follows:

> *CA* for *Centesimus Annus* (1991)
> *LE* for *Laborem Exercens* (1981)
> *SRS* for *Sollicitudo Rei Socialis* (1987)
> *FC* for *Familiaris Consortio* (1981)
> *RH* for *Redemptor Hominis* (1979)

The other **standard source** of Catholic teaching is the revised
edition of *The Catechism of the Catholic Church* (London:
Geoffrey Chapman, 1999). The sections most directly about
Catholic Social Teaching will be found in Part Three.

Other important documents include the teaching documents of
the Catholic **Bishops' Conference** of England and Wales, such
as *The Common Good (1996)* and *Vote for the Common Good
(2001)*, as well as *A Spirituality of Work (2001)* from the
Committee for the World of Work.

Important anthologies of CST documents include:
D.J. O'Brien and T.A. Shannon, *Catholic Social Thought: The
Documentary Heritage* (Maryknoll, NY: Orbis Books, 1992).
M. Walsh and B. Davies, *Proclaiming Justice and Peace:
Papal Documents from Rerum Novarum through Centesimus
Annus* (Mystic, CT: Twenty-Third Publications, 1991).
Pontifical Council for Justice and Peace, *The Social Agenda: A
Collection of Magisterial Texts* (Libreria Editrice Vaticana, 2000).

A valuable **introduction** to Catholic Social Teaching:
David Albert Jones OP, *Living Life to the Full: An Introduction to the Moral and Social Teaching of the Catholic Church* (Oxford: Family Publications, 2001).

Textbooks
The most complete and rigorous studies of Catholic Social teaching have been made by the Jesuit scholar, Fr Rodger Charles. These also provide the historical context for understanding the development of social doctrine:
Rodger Charles SJ, *Christian Social Witness and Teaching, 2 vols. (Leominster: Gracewing, 1998)*
Rodger Charles SJ, *An Introduction to Catholic Social Teaching (Oxford: Family Publications, 1999)*
Rodger Charles SJ with D. MacLaren OP, *The Social Teaching of Vatican II (San Francisco and Oxford: Ignatius Press and Plater, 1982)*

World Wide Web Resources
For the official Vatican website, containing all the recent documents: *www.vatican.va.*
The *Catholic Encyclopedia*, the *Summa* of St Thomas, and many other useful resources can be found at: *www.newadvent.org.*
An impressive website produced by the Office for Social Justice of the Archdiocese of St Paul and Minneapolis: *www.osjspm.org/cst/.*
The Busy Christian's Guide to Catholic Social Teaching: *www.uscatholic.org/cstline/tline.html.*
A site linked to the Catholic Worker Movement: *www.wctc.net/~mjbach/index.html.*
The home page of CAFOD, the Catholic charity for international aid: *www.cafod.org.uk.*

For Further Study

G.K. Chesterton, *What's Wrong with the World* (San Francisco: Ignatius Press, 1994).

C.S. Lewis, *The Abolition of Man* (London: Harper Collins, 1999).

Servais Pinckaers OP, *Morality: The Catholic View* (South Bend, IN: St Augustine's Press, 2001)

Mary Shivanandan, *Crossing the Threshold of Love: A New Vision of Marriage in the Light of John Paul II's Anthropology* (Edinburgh: T&T Clark, 1999).

CTS
MEMBERSHIP

We hope you have enjoyed reading this booklet. If you would like to read more of our booklets or find out more about CTS - why not do one of the following?

1. Join our Readers CLUB.
We will send you a copy of every new booklet we publish, through the post to your address. You'll get 20% off the price too.

2. Support our work and Mission.
Become a CTS Member. Every penny you give will help spread the faith throughout the world. What's more, you'll be entitled to special offers exclusive to CTS Members.

3. Ask for our Information Pack.
Become part of the CTS Parish Network by selling CTS publications in your own parish.

Call us now on 020 7640 0042 or return this form to us at CTS, 40-46 Harleyford Road, London SE11 5AY
Fax: 020 7640 0046 email: info@cts-online.org.uk

❏ I would like to join the *CTS Readers Club*

❏ Please send me details of how to join CTS as a *Member*

❏ Please send me a *CTS Information Pack*

Name:..

Address:..

....

Post Code:...

Phone:...

email address: ....

Registered charity no. 218951.
Registered in England as a company limited by guarantee no.57374.